The HERSHEY'S Milk Chocolate Bar

Fractions Book

By Jerry Pallotta   Illustrated by Rob Bolster

Cartwheel
B·O·O·K·S®

Scholastic Inc.

New York   Toronto   London   Auckland   Sydney   Mexico City   New Delhi   Hong Kong

A zillion thanks to Karen Spencer of Chesterfield Academy, Joan Schweickert of Woodland Elementary, and Donna Atwood of St. Sebastian's School.

Jerry Pallotta

This book is dedicated to the friendship between Elizabeth and Linda.

Rob Bolster

© 1999 Hershey Foods Corporation.
Trademarks used under license,
Corporate Board Books Licensee.
Text copyright © 1999 Jerry Pallotta.
Illustrations copyright © 1999 Rob Bolster.
All rights reserved. Published by Scholastic Inc.
SCHOLASTIC, CARTWHEEL BOOKS and associated logos
are trademarks and/or registered trademarks of Scholastic Inc.

Library of Congress Cataloging-in-Publication Data available.

ISBN 0-439-13519-2

30 29 28 27   6 7/0

Printed in the U.S.A.
First Scholastic printing, September 1999

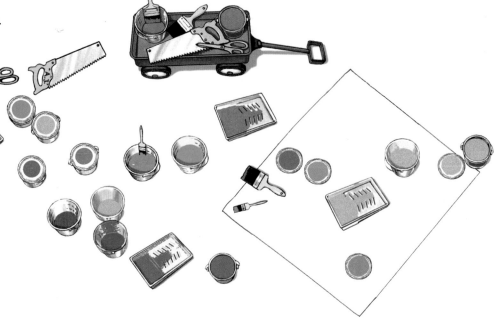

$$\frac{1}{1} = \text{one}$$

Milk chocolate, oooh! Delicious!
Here is a HERSHEY'S milk chocolate bar, the kind Milton Hershey
made famous. Before we eat it, we are going to learn about fractions.

Let's start by taking the wrapper off. Remember not to litter.

one whole **1**

Here we have one whole milk chocolate candy bar.
And what is a fraction? A fraction is a part or a portion of a whole thing.
We are using a HERSHEY'S milk chocolate bar as our whole thing.

$\dfrac{12}{12}$ twelve-twelfths

If you break this candy bar apart, you will see twelve equal sections.
One, two, three, four, five, six, seven, eight, nine, ten, eleven and twelve.

one whole $\frac{12}{12} = \frac{1}{1}$

You can stack the twelve equal sections on top of each other. Hey! It looks different, but any way you rearrange them, they still equal one whole candy bar.

$\dfrac{1}{12}$ one-twelfth

Maybe this is the easiest way to understand fractions. What would you rather eat? One-twelfth of a candy bar?

Or would you rather eat eleven-twelfths of a candy bar? If you love milk chocolate, the answer is simple. As you can see, doing fractions can be fun.

$\dfrac{1}{2}$ one-half

Here is one-half of a HERSHEY'S milk chocolate bar.

six-twelfths $\frac{6}{12}$

And here is the other half. Six-twelfths is equal to one-half. When two fractions equal each other, they are called equivalent fractions.

$$\frac{6}{12} = \frac{1}{2}$$

$\dfrac{1}{3}$  one-third

HERSHEY'S   HERSHEY'S   HERSHEY'S   HERSHEY'S

Here is one-third of a whole HERSHEY'S milk chocolate bar. How did we get to the fraction of one-third? Think of it like this, our candy bar can be divided into three equal groups. Each of the three groups has four sections.

two-thirds $\frac{2}{3}$

What is left over is two-thirds.
One-third plus two-thirds equals three-thirds.
When the top number and the bottom number
are the same, the fraction is equal to one.

$$\frac{1}{3}+\frac{2}{3}=\frac{3}{3}=1$$

$$\frac{4}{12}$$ four-twelfths

$$\frac{4}{12} = \frac{1}{3}$$

Here is another way of saying one-third. Four-twelfths is equal to one-third.

eight-twelfths $\frac{8}{12}$

$$\frac{4}{12} + \frac{8}{12} = \frac{12}{12} = 1$$

And what is left over? Eight-twelfths.
Eight-twelfths is equal to two-thirds.
Four-twelfths plus eight-twelfths equals
twelve-twelfths which equals one whole candy bar.

$\dfrac{1}{4}$ one-fourth

Here is one-fourth of a HERSHEY'S milk chocolate bar. If you want to call this fraction one-quarter, that is okay too!

three-fourths $\dfrac{3}{4}$

Here is what is left over, three-fourths, or you could call it three-quarters.

$$\dfrac{1}{4} + \dfrac{3}{4} = \dfrac{4}{4} = 1$$

$$\frac{3}{12}$$ three-twelfths

$$\frac{3}{12} = \frac{1}{4}$$

Three-twelfths is another way of saying one-fourth. Did you know that the top number of a fraction is called the numerator and the bottom number is called the denominator? Now you know!

nine-twelfths $\frac{9}{12}$

Let's explain it another way.
Three-fourths is equal to nine-twelfths.

$$\frac{3}{12} + \frac{9}{12} = \frac{12}{12} = 1$$

$\dfrac{1}{5}$ one-fifth

It's time for something different. We can still do fractions without the candy bar. There are five cows on this page. Four cows have black spots and one cow has red spots. One-fifth of the cows on this page has red spots.

Did you ever wonder why Hershey's chocolate factory was built in the middle of farm country? There is an easy answer. MILK! One of the three main ingredients used in making milk chocolate is milk.

one-seventh $\dfrac{1}{7}$

moo

moo

moo

moo

moo

moo

If six cows mooed, and you mooed also, your moo would be one-seventh of all of the moos on this page. Don't forget to ignore the duck!

$$\frac{1}{6}$$ one-sixth

$$\frac{2}{12} \div \frac{2}{2} = \frac{1}{6}$$

Back to the candy bar. We need to learn how to put a fraction into its lowest terms.
If you divide the numerator and the denominator by the same factor, you can simplify
this fraction to its lowest terms. One-sixth is the lowest term of two-twelfths.

five-sixths $\dfrac{5}{6}$

Five-sixths is what is left over from a whole candy bar after removing one-sixth.

$$\frac{6}{6} - \frac{1}{6} = \frac{5}{6}$$

$$\frac{2}{12}$$ **two-twelfths**

Here is an equation that is easy to understand.
One-sixth is equal to two-twelfths.

$$\frac{1}{6} = \frac{2}{12}$$

ten-twelfths $\frac{10}{12}$

Here's another way to say five-sixths, ten-twelfths.
It is starting to look more delicious after every fraction we show.

$\dfrac{1}{8}$ one-eighth

It's time for another break.
Chocolate comes from cocoa pods.
The cacao tree grows in very warm and moist
climates. Here are eight pods. If one pod fell off and
bonked you on the head, you would have been bonked
on the head by one-eighth of the cocoa pods on this page.

one-ninth $\dfrac{1}{9}$

Cocoa, milk, and sugar are the three main ingredients used in making milk chocolate. Sugar usually comes from sugar cane. If you cut down one stalk, you will have cut down one-ninth of the sugar canes left on this field.

$$\frac{5}{12}$$ five-twelfths

Here is an interesting fraction. It is already in its lowest terms.
The fraction five-twelfths cannot be broken down or reduced any further.

seven-twelfths $\frac{7}{12}$

The amount left over from five-twelfths is seven-twelfths.
Seven-twelfths is another fraction that is in its lowest terms.

$\dfrac{1}{10}$ one-tenth

Here is a way to get a fraction of one-tenth. There are ten candy bars on this page. One out of the ten candy bars is unwrapped.

thirteen-twelfths $\frac{13}{12}$

Here is a fraction where the top number is larger than the bottom number.
This is called an improper fraction. Thirteen-twelfths is really one and one-twelfth.
Whoever made this fraction used more than one candy bar.

So far in this book, we learned that the main ingredients in milk chocolate are sugar, milk and cocoa. We also learned the fractions: one-twelfth, two-twelfths, three-twelfths, four-twelfths, five-twelfths, six-twelfths, seven-twelfths, eight-twelfths, nine-twelfths, ten-twelfths, eleven-twelfths, twelve-twelfths and even thirteen-twelfths.
We also did fractions of one-half, one-third, one-fourth, one-fifth, one-sixth, one-seventh, one-eighth, one-ninth and one-tenth.

If you want to know what fraction of ingredients are used in making a HERSHEY'S milk chocolate bar, sorry, these fractions are top secret!